TRAPPED
in the
ORGANIZATION
(Fox's Fixations)

by Joe Fox

PRICE/STERN/SLOAN
Publishers, Inc., Los Angeles
1980

Illustrations by Ed Powers

Copyright© 1980 by Joseph M. Fox
Published by Price/Stern/Sloan Publishers, Inc.
410 North La Cienega Boulevard, Los Angeles, California 90048

ISBN: 0-8431-0689-1
Library of Congress Catalog Card No.: 80-80152

CONTENTS

To
John, Bill, Dan,
Mary, Lucy, Paul
&
Lucile

INTRODUCTION

The organization is not insane, despite over-whelming evidence to the contrary. It is incomprehensible to those who have to deal with it, work in it, keep it going, or depend on it to deliver goods.

Most people never realize that the important organization rules are never written down. The written rules are not the important ones.

Why big organizations act the way they do, and how to cope with them and their parts and rules and convoluted workings, are what this book is about.

It might save your sanity!

It might get you promoted!

But don't let the boss – or personnel – see you reading it!

COMMITTEEOLOGY

COMMITTEEOLOGY

The scourge of the twentieth century is not war, or pollution, or the energy crunch – it is the committee!

The committee has been known to drive perfectly sane people over the brink.

Committees are contagious; they have been known to bring countries to complete standstills.

People have been known to retire early rather than to serve on yet another committee.

The committee is not really new; It has been around for centuries. It has simply been ignored by historians because committees have never accomplished anything worth remembering. Has there ever been a monument to a committee? Obviously people would rather just forget about them. Which is precisely why the large organization feels free to use so monstrous a device.

COMMITTEEOLOGY

The Committee:

    is a lightning rod put out by wary executives when they see an approaching storm.

The Committee:

    is a safe way to vent the frustrations of middle-managers by providing the illusion of power.

The Committee:

    gives frustrated employees a chance to be heard - and heard - and heard . . .

The Committee:

    gives the unrecognized a chance to boast.

The Committee:

    gives the weary a chance to sleep.

The Committee:

    gives the voyeurs a chance to watch.

BUREAUCRACY

BUREAUCRACY

Organizations unleash whole galaxies of rules, regulations and policies – all of which ensure that the organization will become a Bureaucracy.

This fixation for tranquility breeds – rules, regulations and rigors . . . standards, structures and strictures . . . the Book, the bureaus, the bureaucrats . . .

The Law is called POLICY.

Policy is contained in "the Book."

The Book is protected by hoards of fiendish nitpickers, called Staff.

Staff believes it is the last defense against that worst of all heresies, Precedent.

A rich organization can perpetuate this kind of procedure for decades.

The code of the organization is stronger and more bizarre than "the code of the hills."

BUREAUCRACY

AXIOM 1   A staff out of control is the boss's fault.

AXIOM 2   The staff goes on and on.

AXIOM 3   The staff will always say that 'it will never work.'

Corollary 1:
   If it does work, they share the spoils. If it doesn't, they told you so.

AXIOM 4   To be safe, move slowly.

Corollary 1:
   To really be safe, do not move at all. Only appear to move.

AXIOM 5   The richer the organization, the more ridiculous the procedures.

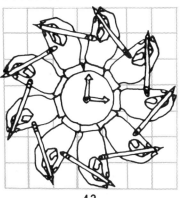

BUREAUCRACY

AXIOM 6   "Positive" should never be used when dealing with a bureaucracy.

AXIOM 7   "Officials are highly educated and onesided, in his own department an official can grasp whole trains of thought from a single word, but let him have something from another department explained to him by the hour -- he may nod politely, but he will understand not a word of it."
                                    —Franz Kafka

AXIOM 8   A bureaucracy can outwait anything.

Corollary 1:
   Never get caught between two bureaucracies.

AXIOM 9   A bureaucracy is a staff out of control.

Corollary 1:
   A staff is a committee out of control.

AXIOM 10   A bureaucracy actually believes it is the real world.

AXIOM 11   A bureaucracy: a group of highly motivated snails.

AXIOM 12   Policy has absolutely nothing to do with reality.

BUREAUCRACY

- The best defense is no defense! To appear impervious to attack is to be so.

- To be always on the defensive is to lose! The opposition need not even attack.

TO SURVIVE IN THE BUREAUCRACY:

1. Bring no problems upward without solutions!

2. Say loyal things – or nothing!

- In a bureaucracy it is more important to keep expense from rising 1% than to increase profit 100%.

- In a bureaucracy, all fights are with internal – not external – rivals.

CONFLICT

CONFLICT

Despite The Organization's desire for Glacial Tranquility, the power and ambition of its people spawn continual conflict.

AXIOM 1   Security and Opportunity are strangers.

AXIOM 2   "He/she who has never been in battle cannot vouch for his/her courage."
                                  —anonymous

AXIOM 3   It is easy to advise.
It is easy to criticize.
It is hard to **do**.

AXIOM 4   The difference between being stubborn and steadfast is whether or not you are right.

AXIOM 5   "What ceases to be a matter of controversy ceases to be a matter of interest."
                                  —anonymous

AXIOM 6   "Courage is grace under pressure."
                                  —Ernest Hemingway

CONFLICT

AXIOM 7   Fight the issue, not the person.
Keep all conflict impersonal.

AXIOM 8   "The best time to win a fight is before it starts."
— Frederick W. Lewis

AXIOM 9   "Never cut what you can untie."
—Joseph Joubert

AXIOM 10   If you must fight, fight to win. Draws are losses.

AXIOM 11   If at all possible, do not fight your boss.

AXIOM 12   Survive first, then do long-term planning.

AXIOM 13   "The difference between iron and steel is fire, and the steel is worth it."
—anonymous

AXIOM 14   "There is no merit where there is no trial, and until experience has stamped her mark, fools may pass as wise men and cowards as heroes."
—anonymous

AXIOM 15   Do not confuse competence and good fortune.

CONFLICT

AXIOM 16   "Adversity makes men; good fortune makes monsters."

—French proverb

AXIOM 17   Courage must sometimes be forced into action by boldness.

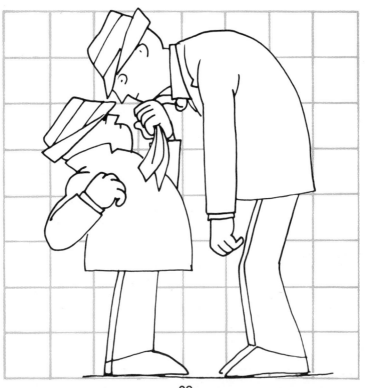

CONFLICT

AXIOM 18   Hierarchies do not foster hostility from below.

AXIOM 19   Large organizations have "mock" conflicts, performed to keep everyone in practice. Do not make the mistake of thinking that these are real. Above all, do not harm anyone in these "mock" conflicts.

AXIOM 20   In very rich organizations style and form are much more important than results.

"When man is fearless he is finished."
— Maurice Maeterlinck

"Man is God afraid."
— anonymous

MANAGEMENT STYLES

MANAGEMENT STYLES

AXIOM 1   "His look is lightning, his word a storm, his vengeance hell. At close quarters he is rather trying."
— J.C. Lavater

AXIOM 2   "You do not lead people by hitting them over the head."
—Dwight Eisenhower

AXIOM 3   To silence dissent, raise the flag.

AXIOM 4   Rich organizations, like rich people, tend toward eccentricity.

AXIOM 5   The high level manager cannot disown those below him.

AXIOM 6   "Everyone knows that it all rests on what name you succeed in imposing on the facts."
—Jerome Cohen

AXIOM 7   "Results count! He is mischievous, paranoid and an old lady – but he's brilliant!
— A chairman of the board

POWER

POWER

The desire for power infects most organizations, and power is not an unmixed blessing!

AXIOM 1   "The real pleasure of power is the pleasure of freedom."
                                           —Robert Heller

AXIOM 2   Two positions in our society bestow absolute power – Chairman of the Board and medical doctor.

AXIOM 3   Chairmen of the Board are told only happy news.

AXIOM 4   Power exiles reality.

AXIOM 5   "Power buries those who wield it."
                                           —Talmud

AXIOM 6   "He did not care in which direction the car was traveling as long as he was in the driver's seat."
                                           —Lord Beaverbrook

AXIOM 7   "A person gets frustrated only if he has choices."
                                           —Don Walsh

POWER

AXIOM 8   "Those who have power are liable to sin more; no theorum in geometry is more certain."
                                              —Gottfried Leibnitz

AXIOM 9   There are four sources of power in today's large organization:
   a.   the executive and his advisors
   b.   the competent doer
   c.   the customer
   d.   the bureaucracy

AXIOM 10   "Power is poison."
                                              —Francis Fenlon

AXIOM 11   "The possession of an unlimited power corrodes the conscience, hardens the heart and confounds the understanding."
                                              —Lord Acton

AXIOM 12   "The true theory of freedom excludes all absolute power."
                                              —Lord Acton

AXIOM 13   Man resists change because he is afraid of the dark.

POWER

AXIOM 14   Arrogance is too often the companion of excellence.

AXIOM 15   "Power is doing what you want when you want and how you want."
                                            —anonymous

AXIOM 16   "Success is a rare paint; it hides all the ugliness."
                                            —Sir John Suckling

AXIOM 17   "When the tide comes in, so does the flotsam and jetsam."
                                            —Carl Wolf

AXIOM 18   Every army –and especially winning ones – has camp followers.

AXIOM 19   Every football team has cheerleaders.

AXIOM 20   Every rich organization has posturing yes-men.

AMBITION

AMBITION

The mainspring of most people is the ambition they hold in their stomachs . . .

It can make people do amazing things, beyond the imagination of the wildest visionary. Ambition can be the cannon you are shot from, or the hair shirt of your entire life! It is probably both!!!

Of course, one does not gain power unless one has ambition.

AXIOM 1   "Happy people are failures because they are on such good terms with themselves, they don't give a damn."
                                    —Agatha Christie

AXIOM 2   "Whenever men are not obliged to fight from necessity, they fight from ambition."
                                    —Niccolo Machiavelli

             Corollary 1:
                 Are you ambitious? Will you move to New York?

AXIOM 3   "Though ambition is itself a vice, it is often the parent of virtues."
                                    —Marcus Fabrius Quintilian

AMBITION

AXIOM 4   "Avarice, ambition, lust etc. are species of madness."
—Baruch Spinoza

AXIOM 5   "Ambition without conscience is an untamed beast."
—Robert G. Ingersoll

AXIOM 6   "Ambition: The moral flabbiness born of excessive worship of the bitch goddess, Success."
—Henry James

AXIOM 7   "Try not to be a man of success; try to be a man of value."
—Albert Einstein

AXIOM 8   "My intentions were completely dishonorable–that I went straight is simply the measure of my incompetence."
—anonymous

AXIOM 9   "I could do great things if I were not so busy doing little things."
—anonymous

WORKAHOLICS

WORKAHOLICS

But ambition can get out of control, and the result is the scourge of the organization, The Workaholic!

AXIOM 1   Workaholics should be treated, not promoted.

AXIOM 2   My boss acts like he's in the Grand Prix – and I am the car.

AXIOM 3   "So much of what we call management consists of making it hard for people to do their job."
—Peter Drucker

AXIOM 4   Workaholics never have enough on their plates; their subordinates always have too much.

Corollary 1:
"The human race has been playing at children's games from the beginning, and will probably do so till the end, which is a great nuisance for the few people who grow up."
—G.K. Chesterton

DECISIVENESS

DECISIVENESS

Perhaps the opposite of the committee is the decisive manager! Epitomized by the World War II movie heroes, the decisive manager is a true American institution! We all aspire to grab a few facts and zap! Make a decision and zap! It is the only decision that could have been made to make everything all right. That happens in the movies but not very often in the real world. Let us look at the area of being decisive and see how it is handled in the organization.

Many people believe that decisiveness is essential to the exercise of power, but...

AXIOM 1   Decisiveness is not in itself a virtue.

AXIOM 2   "My policy is to have no policy."
                                —Abraham Lincoln

AXIOM 3   Decisiveness for the sake of itself is a runaway bulldozer.

AXIOM 4   Hindsight, unless it is on your own actions, is like history: we know the end before we know the beginning and therefore we can never know the beginning the way it truly was.

DECISIVENESS

AXIOM 5 To decide not to decide is a decision.
To fail to decide is a failure.

AXIOM 6 "Some questions cannot be answered, but they can be decided."
—Harry S Truman

AXIOM 7 Advocates rest content that they argued well; deciders must live with their decisions.

AXIOM 8 Every decision is a risk.

AXIOM 9 Most managers do not want to decide; they want strong reasons for your decisions.

AXIOM 10 A leader must know, must know that he knows, and must show that he knows.

AXIOM 11 "He built that plant without approval and everyone was mad as hell at him – for an hour."
—A chairman of the board

AXIOM 12 "He will not give in to the cry 'let's make another study.' That is the coward's way."
—Peter Drucker

DECISIVENESS

AXIOM 13   An important reason for an executive's existence is to make sensible exceptions to policy.

AXIOM 14   "Success is the child of audacity."
                                        —Benjamin Disraeli

AXIOM 15   "He advanced slowly into the silence and made it verbal. . . . consider the courage in all of that."
                                        —Howard Nemeroy

AXIOM 16   "For purposes of action, nothing is more useful than narrowness of thought combined with energy of will."
                                        —Henri Frederick Amile

AXIOM 17   "(Action) is the last resource of those who do not know how to dream."
                                        —Oscar Wilde

AXIOM 18   "Yesterday I dared to struggle;
                today I dare to win."
                                        —Bernadette Devlin

FUNCTIONAL DEPARTMENTS

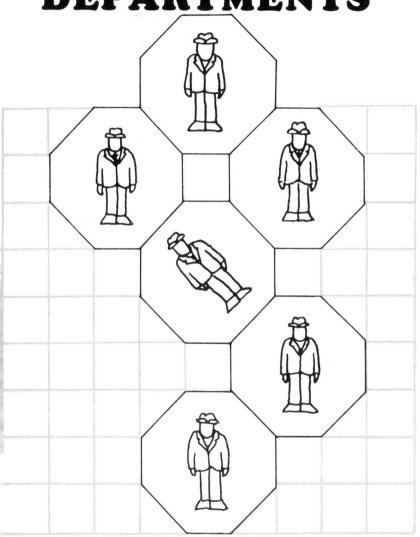

FUNCTIONAL DEPARTMENTS

The organizationalists approach these organizations by examining one of the methods universally used to keep things Tranquil. Organization! Departments! And with the Departments, levels! Keep everything ordered and orderly and quiet!

The functional departments within all large organizations are not only the same in name, they are the same in behavior. They are utterly predictable!

THINGS THAT CAN BE COUNTED ON IN A CRISIS:

- **Marketing** says yes.
- **Finance** says no.
- **Legal** has to review it.
- **Personnel** is concerned.
- **Planning** is frantic.
- **Engineering** is above it all.
- **Manufacturing** needs more floor space.
- **Top Management** wants someone responsible.

FUNCTIONAL DEPARTMENTS

AXIOM 1   Almost all executives are Administrators; very few are Entrepreneurs.

AXIOM 2   Whoever first called the parts of an organization "divisions" was prophetic.

AXIOM 3   Ask a lawyer for an opinion only after you tell him what you want the answer to be.

AXIOM 4   "There's no better way of exercising the imagination than the study of law. No poet ever interpreted nature as freely as a lawyer interprets truth."
           —Jean Giraudoux

AXIOM 5   Lawyers would rather be smart than effective.

AXIOM 6   Ph.Ds would rather look for things than find them.

AXIOM 7   "Finance: The art of passing money from hand to hand until it finally disappears."
           —anonymous

AXIOM 8   "Stroking a financial man is like petting a cobra."
           —anonymous

FUNCTIONAL DEPARTMENTS

AXIOM 9

"The most common cause of executive failure is unwillingness to change with the demands of a new position."

—Peter Drucker

AXIOM 10

Planning:
"If you don't know where you are going, any road will get you there."

—Lewis Carroll

Corollary 1:
"If you don't know where you are going, you'll wind up someplace else."

—Lawrence Peter

Corollary 2:
Planning: 15 people in a car going 90 miles an hour, and everyone is looking out the rear window.

AXIOM 11

Darwin's Law of Natural Selection explains why a good factory manager can't sell anything, and why a good sales manager couldn't run a bicycle shop!

AXIOM 12

A lawyer never really wants the client to understand the strategy – it takes away the mystery.

FUNCTIONAL DEPARTMENTS

AXIOM 13   Time to coordinate approvals goes up as the nth power of the number of signatures required. Complicated things never get coordinated.

AXIOM 14   The judge must decide; all the advocate must do is argue well. The general manager is the judge; the functional vice presidents the advocates.

THE THINGS THAT FUNCTIONAL DEPARTMENTS ARE ENAMOURED WITH ARE WELL KNOWN:

Personnel	loves "the book"
Marketing	loves "the customer"
Legal	loves "the law"
Accounting	loves "the numbers"
Computerniks	love "the random numbers"
Finance	loves "the money"
Engineering	loves "the complexity"

LEVELOLOGY

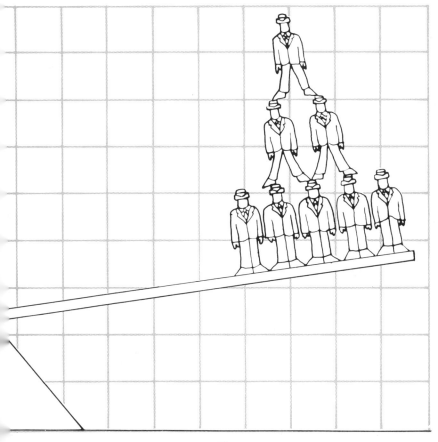

LEVELOLOGY

People in the middle ages thought they would fall off the end of the earth if they went too far to sea. Today some people still believe that the rules of behavior in large organizations are the same for all levels of management. Of course they are wildly different! Top management lives better than most kings of all times and have tremendous power and privileges. Middle managers are like nobility; managers like landed gentry, and employees like serfs.

What will get you promoted at one level will get you killed at another. Let us look at the levels within the organization and learn about the convoluted opportunities that lie therein.

AXIOM 1   Top management is the king's castle. Middle management is the war zone. First-line management is the trenches.

AXIOM 2   Too much reality in the castle is usually fatal.

       Corollary 1:
         Don't tell God not to take Himself too seriously.

       Corollary 2:
         Don't tell God He needs the angels.

AXIOM 3   An executive manages; he doesn't do.

       Corollary 1:
         You'll know you're in top management when you are doing all the work.

LEVELOLOGY

AXIOM 4   The curse of middle management: Top management will always believe some stranger they meet on a plane before they will believe their own staff.

Corollary 1:
You can't be that good; you work for me.

Corollary 2:
"I wouldn't belong to any club that would have me."
— Groucho Marx

Corollary 3:
"Why should we not trust strangers? They have not yet disappointed us."
— variation of
Samuel Johnson

AXIOM 5   "Middle management in a declining company is like a deck chair on the Titanic."
— anonymous

AXIOM 6   You can tell the level of a man by the cost of his toys.

AXIOM 7   "An executive is anyone making more than $30,000 and not related to the chairman."
— anonymous

AXIOM 8   When the elephants are fighting, stay out of the clearing.

LEVELOLOGY

AXIOM 9

In all large organizations, there are only two types of people:

Egos and Super-Egos. You can tell them apart as follows:

a) Egos consider nothing impossible.

b) Super-Egos consider nothing impossible for you.

REALITY

REALITY

We have seen how power can banish reality. But even in the large organization, reality will occasionally raise its unwelcome head. When it does it can cause uproar, confusion and chaos. And if you are ready for it, you can even benefit.

AXIOM 1
"Nothing matters very much, and very few things matter at all."
—Lord Balfour

AXIOM 2
What you think depends on the hat you wear.

AXIOM 3
"Nice guy": "Not tough"

AXIOM 4
"My grandfather always said that living is like licking honey off a thorn."
—Louis Adamic

AXIOM 5
The problem with being a success is that you must continue to be a success.

AXIOM 6
"Humankind cannot bear too much reality."
—anonymous

AXIOM 7
"It is useless for the sheep to pass resolutions in favor of vegetarianism while the wolf remains of a different opinion."
—anonymous

REALITY

AXIOM 8   "Reality: A gang of brutal facts killing a beautiful theory."

—variation of
Thomas Huxley

AXIOM 9   "All men dream but not equally. Those who dream by night in the dusty recesses of their minds wake in the day to find that it was vanity; but the dreamers of the day are dangerous for they may act their dream with open eyes, to make it possible."

—T. E. Lawrence

AXIOM 10   "It is not enough that we do our best; we must do what is necessary."

—Winston S. Churchill

AXIOM 11   The first mission of the management of a successful company is to preserve.

Corollary 1:
"At every crossway on the road that leads to the future, each progressive spirit is opposed by a thousand men appointed to guard the past."

—Maurice Maeterlink

Corollary 2:
Nothing impedes like success.

REALITY

AXIOM 12   A large organization is a hostile setting and all presentations are designed to fend off questions.

AXIOM 13   "Those who mistake their good luck for their merit are inevitably headed for disaster."
—J. Christopher Herold

AXIOM 14   "Hope is generally a poor guide, though it is very good company along the way."
—George Savile

AXIOM 15   "Error is often more earnest than truth."
—Benjamin Disraeli

AXIOM 16   Management always wants simple answers to complex questions, but there are few simple answers.

AXIOM 17   "The problem with a Harvard-type program is the arrogance it breeds. Students do not learn how difficult it is to accomplish anything."
—Peter Drucker

AXIOM 18   When a problem goes away, the people working to solve it do not.

REALITY

AXIOM 19   Large organizations abhor publicity they do not control.

AXIOM 20   We have made being a manager an end in itself. "What do you want to manage?" A Ph.D. in math responds, "Anything."

AXIOM 21   "An important art of the politician is to find new names for institutions which under old names have become odious to the public."
                                    —Perigord Talleyrand

AXIOM 22   Never be first! Pioneers get killed a lot.

AXIOM 23   Organizations should work independent of personalities, but they don't.

AXIOM 24   "A good slogan can stop analysis for fifty years."
                                    —Wendell Willkie

AXIOM 25   Subordinates of an executive-in-trouble don't want to be sucked down in his wake.

AXIOM 26   "A critic is a man who knows the way but can't drive the car."
                                    —Kenneth Tynan

REALITY

AXIOM 27 "Every so often we pass laws repealing human nature."

—Russell Crouse

AXIOM 28 "Work smarter, not harder" is a losing slogan; top management is doing both.

AXIOM 29 There are jobs in which you can never be a hero, but in which you can be a bum. Running the annual convention is one. Do everything right and you are doing what is expected, foul up and you are dead.

AXIOM 30 Every field of endeavor has its own shorthand to lubricate the movement of its progress. To use this jargon with the uninitiated is to insult them.

AXIOM 31 The first 25% of any large meeting is spent in venting and puffing. Venting is blowing off steam, expending frustration.
Puffing is portraying an exterior that is a size bigger than reality. Therefore schedule all important items for the second half of the meeting.

AXIOM 32 "We mount to heaven on the ruins of our cherished dreams, finding in the end that our failures were successes after all."

—Amos B. Alcott

REALITY

AXIOM 33 Brochuremanship: The paper ship/computer/ anything will always out perform the present real article.

AXIOM 34 "A basic myth of management: that success equals skill."
                                    —Robert Heller

AXIOM 35 A general sees peace as the statesman's plot.

AXIOM 36 "Thunder is good, thunder is impressive, but it is lightning that does the work."
                                    —Mark Twain

AXIOM 37 Most are successes and do not know it.

AXIOM 38 "Any technology sufficiently advanced looks like magic."
                                    — Arthur C. Clarke

AXIOM 39 Sincerity and dedication are not necessarily virtues. Herman Goerring had both.

AXIOM 40 "All that I learned there was Latin and lying."
                                    —Herman Hesse re: school

REALITY

AXIOM 41   Compromise is reality. "If you want to hear a pretty speech, go see Lehman. If you want to see how things get done, stay with me."

        —Lyndon B. Johnson to
        a reporter in 1955

AXIOM 42   Anticipation cheats Appreciation!

FIXES FOR EMPLOYEES

FIXES FOR EMPLOYEES

Presented here are the Fixes, a long list of ideas and practices that may be helpful to individuals in the organization.

AXIOM 1   Being an owner is all in your head.

Corollary 1:
Management is not doing you a favor in giving you a job.

AXIOM 2   Undue reverence is a sign of psychosis.

Corollary 1:
There are no big guys, only guys.

AXIOM 3   There is nothing so disheartening as the stupidity of a superior.

Corollary 1:
'Follow the leader' is a child's game.

AXIOM 4   Work is ennobling, but get paid.

AXIOM 5   What you will be you are becoming today.

FIXES FOR EMPLOYEES

AXIOM 6   The boss will be the boss, so you might as well take credit for letting him be the boss.

AXIOM 7   No one likes to be wrong, not even the boss.

AXIOM 8   Treat everyone as your equal.

> Corollary 1:
> "Never be haughty to the humble;
> never be humble to the haughty."
> —Jefferson Davis

> Corollary 2:
> "When dealing with someone important, picture him in his pajamas."
> —Joe Kennedy

AXIOM 9   We are launched down the ways like ships. It takes courage, not brains, to get off the ways.

AXIOM 10   Your opinion versus the boss's, loses.

> Corollary 1:
> If you must fight the boss, use facts.

AXIOM 11   Be negative very positively.

FIXES FOR EMPLOYEES

AXIOM 12   If you cannot produce results, show furious activity.

Corollary 1:
To Snow: To show evidence of hard work as a substitute for understanding.

Corollary 2:
To Dazzle: To show evidence of understanding as a substitute for hard work.

AXIOM 13   FIRST LAW OF POLITICS: stay in with the outs.
FIRST LAW: stay in with everyone.

Corollary 1:
"Always make whatever you are lost in look as much like home as possible."
— Bernard Baruch

AXIOM 14   "See how smart I am" is a loser script.

Corollary 1:
"See how smart I am" comes across as "See how dumb you are."

AXIOM 15   If you don't give a damn you'll probably do better

AXIOM 16   There is never enough time.

FIXES FOR EMPLOYEES

AXIOM 17   "Winning the battle and losing the war." If you don't know what that means, stay home.

AXIOM 18   Get along with your peers; some day one of you will be the boss.

AXIOM 19   The fact that one is in the top job does not mean that he is in control.

AXIOM 20   Eternal vigilance lets you keep your job.

AXIOM 21   Rest on your laurels and you may never move again.

AXIOM 22   The boss is to be told the bad news even if he cannot take it.

Corollary 1:
   Seek criticism when your authority thwarts it.

Corollary 2:
   "Fortune when she caresses a man too much makes him a fool."
                              — Publius Syrus

FIXES FOR EMPLOYEES

AXIOM 23

"The test of a first-rate intelligence is the ability to hold in the mind at the same time two opposed ideas, and still retain the ability to function."
— F. Scott Fitzgerald

FIXES FOR EMPLOYEES

AXIOM 24   "Strong people have strong weaknesses"
                                          —Peter Drucker

Corollary 1:
    "Too" in front of any good trait makes it a weakness.

AXIOM 25   The good guys not only don't always win, they frequently don't get in the game.

Corollary 1:
    'Not fair' is a child's phrase.

Corollary 2:
    "God is not a cosmic bellboy."
                                          —Harry Emerson Fosdick

AXIOM 26   "We judge others on what they have done; we judge ourselves on what we feel capable of doing."
                                          —anonymous

AXIOM 27   "Patience, n.: a minor form of dispair disguised as a virtue."

                                          —Ambrose Bierce

AXIOM 28   "A flawed diamond is better than a perfect brick."
                                          —anonymous

What if you're trying to build a house? KLL

FIXES FOR EMPLOYEES

AXIOM 29   Treat everyone the same and you'll drive out the best.

AXIOM 30   Will he fit with the team? Would Einstein?

AXIOM 31   "It did not do Gen. Wavell any harm to be known as a fairly good minor English poet. At Sears Roebuck it would kill you."

—Peter Drucker

AXIOM 32   When giving advice, seek to help, not to please.

AXIOM 33   Do not tell the boss what to do; tell him what to consider.

Corollary 1:
"Until you have trod the road, advise not the wayside folk."

—Rudyard Kipling

AXIOM 34   Activity is not progress;
hard work is not results.

AXIOM 35   Form is often as important as essence.

FIXES FOR EMPLOYEES

AXIOM 36   People tend to do what they like to do, not necessarily what they are good at.

Corollary 1:
"If the only tool you have is a hammer, you tend to see every problem as a nail."
— Abraham Maslow

AXIOM 37   Do not confuse intentions with ability – especially your own.

AXIOM 38   "Management as a profession has never caught up altogether with another powerful nonvisible force...namely, feelings."
— Harry Levinson

AXIOM 39   For results, use people's strengths. To help people get ahead, work on their weaknesses.

AXIOM 40   If you would know your faults, enumerate your great strengths.

AXIOM 41   "Success is doing what you want, when you want, how you want."
— anonymous

AXIOM 42   Attach yourself to an unsolvable problem.

FIXES FOR EMPLOYEES

AXIOM 43   If they all agree, they cannot all be experts.

AXIOM 44   "Kingham made a habit of telling all his acquaintances sooner or later, what he thought of them – which was invariably disagreeable. He called this process a 'clearing of the atmosphere.'"
                —Aldous Huxley

AXIOM 45   "It was not until quite late in life that I learned how easy it was to say 'I don't know.'"
                —Somerset Maugham

YESMANSHIP

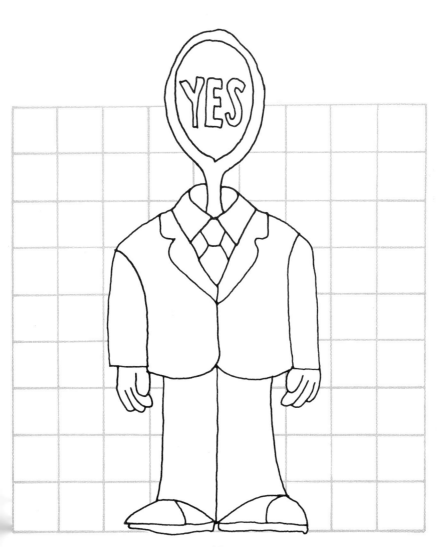

YESMANSHIP

Ever since Og told his boss that "you can beat that polar bear," high level managers have been surrounding themselves with people who know how to say nice things.

Most organizations have staying power, and the results of this kind of nonsense may not be noticed by outsiders for decades.

The fixation for Glacial Tranquility gives rise to hoards of yesmen.

AXIOM 1   The accomplished 'yesman' shows no sign of personal opinion until the leader has given some hints of the direction.

Corollary 1:
Great yesmen show continual evidence of being on both sides.

AXIOM 2   Always let your subordinate give the presentation. Then you can disown it and even him or her if it goes badly.

AXIOM 3   After the boss has stated a position, explain all the things that could go wrong. You are then safe.

AXIOM 4   Beware a person who never dissents.

YESMANSHIP

AXIOM 5   Policy is the large corporation's religion.

AXIOM 6   The large organization wants its people to be ferocious competitors outside and docile followers inside.

AXIOM 7   If you must choose between being competent and embarrassing the boss, be incompetent.

AXIOM 8   Quote people a lot, especially the chairman.

AXIOM 9   You can always disown a quote if it goes awry. After all, someone else said it.

AXIOM 10   It is worth scheming to be the bearer of good news.

Corollary 1:
Don't be in the building when bad news arrives.

AXIOM 11   Are the cheerleaders more highly rewarded than the players?

AXIOM 12   Raise questions and problems ONLY if you have the solutions.

YESMANSHIP

AXIOM 13   "Heresy is the name given to the doctrines of the weak."
                                    —Robert Ingersoll

AXIOM 14   The insecure prattle about 'loyalty.'

AXIOM 15   To select the wrong person for a job is a common mistake; not to remove him/her is a fatal weakness.

AXIOM 16   Antidotes to Yesmanship:
               Choose results over appearances, independence over obedience, the opinionated over the docile, one-sidedness over no-sidedness.

AXIOM 17   "I don't want any yesmen around me. I want people who tell me the truth even though it costs them their jobs."
                                    —Samuel Goldwyn

AXIOM 18   "There's no deodorant like success."
                                    —Elizabeth Taylor

AXIOM 19   Inscrutability: Never let your face shout what you'd never let your lips utter.

YESMANSHIP

AXIOM 20
"The face is the artless index of the mind."
—anonymous

AXIOM 21
"Of all the things you wear, the most important is your expression."
—John Glaskin

AXIOM 22
"Show me any 40 year old who is not responsible for his face."
—Abraham Lincoln

AXIOM 23
"Diplomacy is the art of saying "nice doggie" until you can find a rock."
—Wynn Catlin

FOUR GRAND FIXATIONS

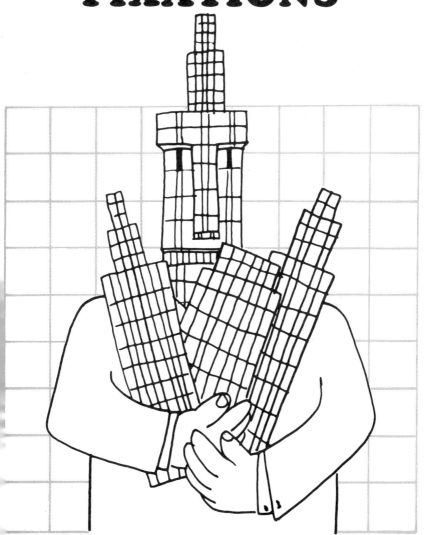

FOUR GRAND FIXATIONS

All large organizations are afflicted with four overpowering obsessions.

The Lust for Intergalactic Power

The large organization is driven to control everything – and this affliction spreads to its managers.

The Passion for Glacial Tranquility

Not even good surprises are welcome, as they are evidence of lack of total control.

The Belief of Global Purpose

What is good for us is obviously good for everybody – and whoever disagrees with us is either confused or evil or both.

The Illusion of Gorgeous Uniqueness

No other organization is like us; were we to disappear, the world would never be the same.

Wouldn't that be _____ !

If you have an organizational epigram of your own and would like it to be considered for a follow-up edition of **Trapped in the Organization,** send it to:

PRICE/STERN/SLOAN *Publishers, Inc.*
410 North La Cienega Boulevard, Los Angeles, California 90048

This book is published by

PRICE/STERN/SLOAN
Publishers, Inc., Los Angeles

whose other splendid titles include such literary classics as:

MURPHY'S LAW AND OTHER REASONS
WHY THINGS GO WRONG! ($2.50)
MURPHY'S LAW / BOOK TWO ($2.50)
THE LEGAL GUIDE TO MOTHER GOOSE ($2.50)
HOW TO BE A JEWISH MOTHER ($2.50)
HOW TO BE AN ITALIAN ($2.50)
THE PROFIT by Kehlog Albran ($2.50)

and many, many more

They are available wherever books are sold, or may be
ordered directly from the publisher by sending check or
money order for total amount plus 50 cents for handling and
mailing. For a complete list of titles send a stamped, self-
addressed envelope **to:**

PRICE/STERN/SLOAN *Publishers, Inc.*
410 North La Cienega Boulevard, Los Angeles, California 90048